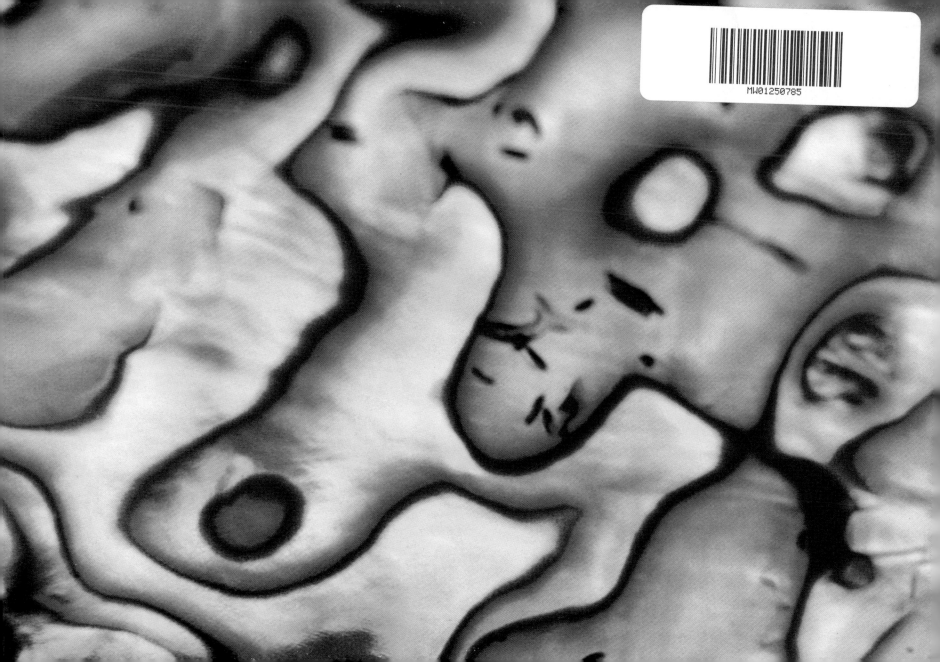

New Zealand

A Nature Lover's Souvenir

For Rachel and Jamie, with love and thanks

Published in 1999 by New Holland Kowhai
an imprint of New Holland Publishers (NZ) Ltd
Auckland • Sydney • London • Cape Town

218 Lake Road, Northcote, Auckland, New Zealand
14 Aquatic Drive, Frenchs Forest, NSW 2086, Australia
24 Nutford Place, London W1H 6DQ, United Kingdom
80 McKenzie Street, Cape Town 8001, South Africa

ISBN: 1 877246 18 2

Managing editor: Renée Lang
Book design: Graeme Leather
Colour reproduction by Colour Symphony Pte Ltd
Printed by Craft Print Pte Ltd, Singapore

FRONT COVER: A jewelled gecko captures its prey amongst
purple mahoe berries.
BACK COVER (FROM LEFT TO RIGHT): View across a small glacial lake on the
Tasman Glacier, Mt Cook National Park; black tree fern in the Karamea
forest, north east of Westport in the South Island.
INSIDE BACK COVER FLAP: The purple-pink flowers of the poroporo, found
on the Three Kings Islands, north west of Cape Maria van Diemen.
END PAPERS: Detail of a paua shell.
TITLE PAGE: The bright yellow flowers of the kowhai, regarded as
New Zealand's national flower.
OPPOSITE: A tangle of kiekie vines growing in a Westland rainforest.

Introduction

Journeying south through the islands of the Pacific, travellers will eventually reach the New Zealand archipelago. But if they are expecting a paradise coloured by warm seas and coral beaches, their first impressions of these shores may come as a surprise. These 'south-sea islands' have snow-capped mountains, glacial-fed rivers, deep lakes, and cold seas hosting penguins, seals and great whales. The ancient rainforests are sanctuary for birds as strange as any to be found in distant lands, yet there are also volcanoes as young and active as any in the Pacific and even swaying palms (the southernmost in the world). New Zealand is also home to a host of unusual and fascinating plants and animals. So, for nature loving travellers every-where, here is a souvenir from an island paradise.

View across a small glacial lake on the Tasman Glacier, Mt Cook National Park.

LEFT: A friendly bottle-nosed dolphin in the Bay of Islands.

RIGHT: Two male sealions keeping company, Otago Peninsula. Sealions can be viewed on a number of Otago and Southland beaches.

LEFT: A downy mollymawk chick sits atop its nest on one of the sub-Antarctic Bounty Islands.

RIGHT: A killer whale glides by underwater in the Hauraki Gulf.

OVERLEAF: Pancake Rocks, Punakaiki, an example of limestone carved by the solvent action of rain water.

LEFT: The seedheads of spinifex roll across the dunes like
   tumbleweeds.

RIGHT: The ramshorn shell is the delicate internal skeleton of a
   tiny nautilus and is often washed up on northern beaches.

OVERLEAF: A pair of gannets beside their cliff top nest at the
   edge of the extensive Cape Kidnappers breeding colony
   (shown opposite) on the east coast of the North Island.

LEFT: A New Zealand flax swamp bordered by native bush and cabbage trees.

OVERLEAF: Splashed in red, pohutukawa trees herald high summer on a northern coast, while (opposite) a lighter shade of red signals a warning from another coastal resident, New Zealand's poisonous katipo spider.

RIGHT: A small group of Snares crested penguins head down to the sea on one of the Snares Islands, south of Stewart Island.

LEFT: The eye of the distinctive yellow-eyed penguin. These penguins can be viewed coming ashore on several Otago and Southland beaches.

PREVIOUS PAGES: A group of southern black-backed gulls gather on the coast of the Otago Peninsula. On the same coast the radiate limpet (opposite) resists a battering from the southern ocean by clinging to the rocks.

Delicate pink jewel anemones (above) and a bright-orange tooth star (right) provide
a splash of colour beneath the waves of Blueskin Bay, just north of Dunedin.

PREVIOUS PAGES: Boulder Beach, on the Otago Peninsula, is a typical landing beach for
several species of seals and penguins seeking shelter from the southern ocean.

RIGHT: A female wandering albatross returns to her large downy chick amongst the windswept tussock of a sub-Antarctic island, while a mother Caspian tern (opposite) feeds her two youngsters on a northern beach.

OVERLEAF: The stark volcanic landscape of White Island echoes a time of great upheaval in the Bay of Plenty. On a nearby island another reminder of New Zealand's distant past, the tuatara (opposite), shares its burrow with a fairy prion.

Close up detail of a carpet of moss and clubmoss, whose windborne spores are carried far and wide to colonise barren land.

LEFT: Both pohutukawa and the Poor Knights Lily are native plant species whose windborne seeds are light enough to cross ocean gaps and colonise northern islands, such as the Poor Knights.

ABOVE: The red-tailed tropicbird is a tropical ocean wanderer occasionally seen in the skies of New Zealand's Far North region.

LEFT: The sight of a white kiwi is a once in a lifetime experience. This young female lives on the island sanctuary of Little Barrier (right), 90 km northwest of Auckland.

OVERLEAF: The tall rimu trees and other podocarps in the Whirinaki forest (on the North Island's east coast) have changed little since the time when dinosaurs walked the earth. Today you would be lucky to catch a glimpse of the rare short-tailed bat (opposite) scampering across the forest floor after dark.

Left: The creamy white flowers of the *Tecomanthe* vine from the Three Kings Islands share the forest with poroporo (right), whose purple-pink flowers are paler than the mainland variety.

Overleaf: Soft tree ferns proliferate under the canopy of many New Zealand forests.

LEFT: A male Archey's frog on the Coromandel Peninsula guards a cluster of precious eggs until they hatch, while a female brown kiwi (right) awaits the return of her own mate. He too will guard her egg until it hatches.

OVERLEAF: A grove of nikau palms in the moonlight on the South Island's West Coast.

LEFT: The crimson-pink flowers of napuka and the scarlet flowers of kaka beak (right) are popular natives with New Zealand gardeners.

PREVIOUS PAGE: Manuka blooms in the bright sunlight of a North Island wetland, above a carpet of umbrella fern.

LEFT: The dense tangled undergrowth of a North Island rainforest is home to the kokako (right), seen here examining forest toadstools the same colour as its bright blue wattles.

PREVIOUS PAGES: Detail of the distinctive pattern found inside the trunk of the mamaku, or black tree fern.

LEFT: A grove of large matai trees on a Southland farm, and the massive square trunk of a kauri on the Coromandel Peninsula (right) are both reminders of the giant trees once common in our forests.

OVERLEAF: The nectar-loving tui (left), and the fruit-eating kereru or woodpigeon (right), are two native birds responsible for pollinating flowers and distributing seeds in a healthy forest.

The dark mossy interior of a southern beech forest in Fiordland.

Above: The sombre coloured kaka, or forest parrot, has a liquid whistle and a weakness for the sweet nectar of crimson rata flowers (right).

Overleaf: Misty cloud-forests deep in the heart of Fiordland (left) were once the last mainland haunt of the kakapo (right), a secretive nocturnal parrot now confined to one or two offshore islands.

PREVIOUS PAGES: A curtain of beautiful but sticky threads strung across a mossy bank may snare an insect meal for the New Zealand glow-worm.

LEFT: The bright red and yellow under-wings of the kea, or mountain parrot, stand out against the bright blue sky.

RIGHT: Cabbage trees, seen here at sunset, are a common feature on hillsides throughout New Zealand.

OVERLEAF: A pair of blue ducks and their brood negotiate a turbulent mountain torrent.

PREVIOUS PAGE: A naturally sculpted limestone outcrop at Castle Hill, Canterbury.

THIS PAGE: Throughout New Zealand, the grey warbler's musical trill heralds spring.

OVERLEAF: Winter icicles hang from a frozen mountain waterfall.

LEFT: The colourful plumage of the takahe seems almost out of place in the mountains, where the subtler colours of a Mount Cook sunset (right) seem more appropriate.

PREVIOUS PAGE: A spray of mountain flax flowers signals a hot alpine summer.

LEFT: Icicles hang from the branch of a southern beech tree, and a penwiper (right) flowers on a scree slope, Marlborough, South Island.

PREVIOUS PAGES: Glaciers such as this one at the head of the Dart Valley add a spectacular vista to the South Island's Southern Alps.

OVERLEAF: An early morning view of Mitre Peak, Fiordland, on an overcast day.